ROA
DE/
NATIONAL PARK

MW01533701

Barbara and Robert Decker

Maps and Drawings by Rick Hazlett

Designed by Kristi Carlson

Printed by Dumont Printing
Fresno, California

Published by Double Decker Press
4087 Silver Bar Road
Mariposa, California 95338

Second Edition © 1996   ISBN: 0-9621019-9-0

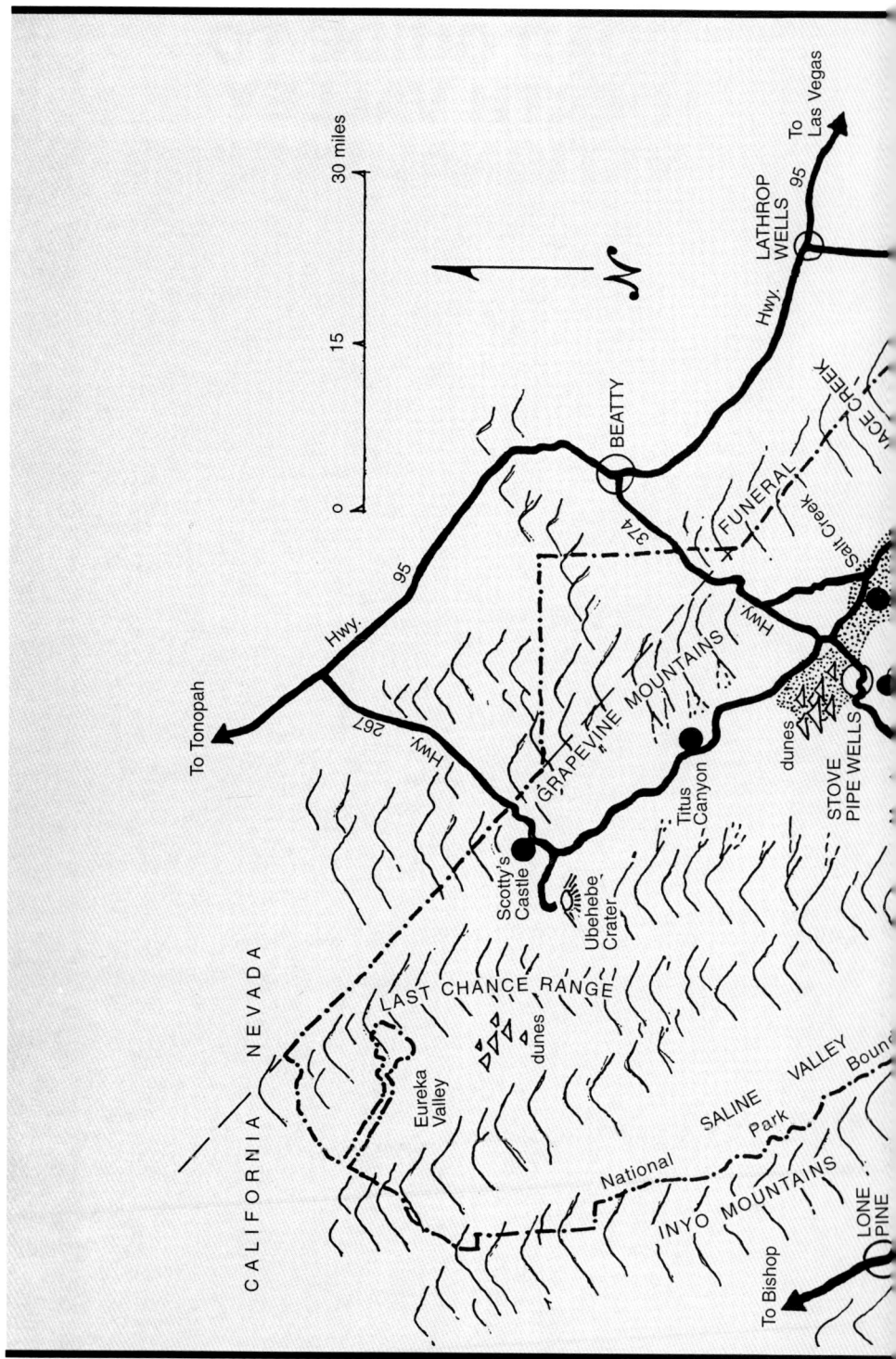

30 miles

15

0

To Las Vegas

LATHROP
WELLS

95

Hwy.

BEATTY

374

FUNERAL

Salt Creek

95

Hwy.

Hwy.

To Tonopah

267

Hwy.

GRAPEVINE MOUNTAINS

dunes

STOVE
PIPE WELLS

Titus
Canyon

Scotty's
Castle

Ubehebe
Crater

LAST CHANCE RANGE

dunes

Eureka
Valley

SALINE VALLEY

Park

Bound

National

INYO MOUNTAINS

LONE
PINE

To Bishop

CALIFORNIA NEVADA

2

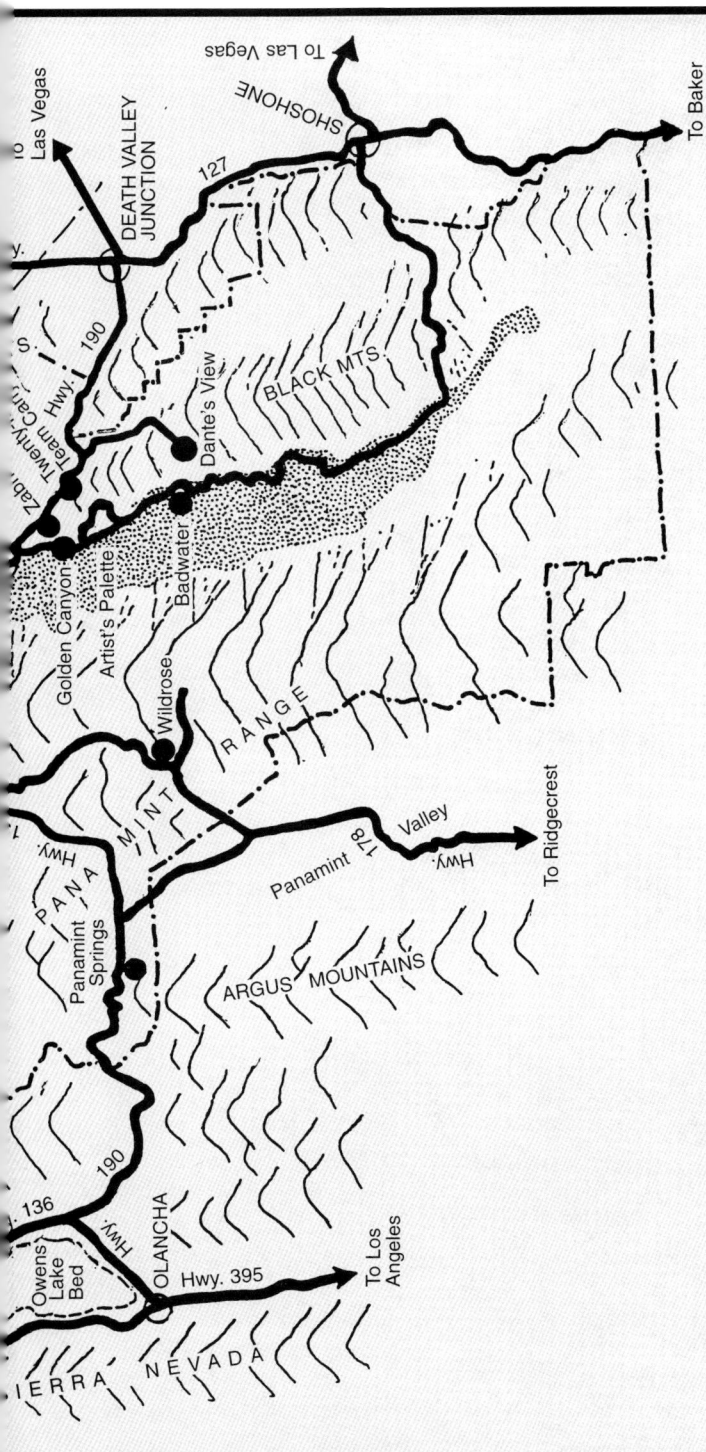

DEATH VALLEY NATIONAL PARK
Dotted pattern shows area below sea level

To Las Vegas

SHOSHONE

To Baker

DEATH VALLEY JUNCTION

To Las Vegas

127

190 Hwy.

Twenty-Team Cany.

Zab...

Dante's View

BLACK MTS

Golden Canyon

Artist's Palette

Badwater

Wildrose

RANGE

P A N A M I N T

Valley

Panamint 178

Hwy.

To Ridgecrest

PANA Hwy.

Panamint Springs

ARGUS MOUNTAINS

190

136

OLANCHA

Owens Lake Bed

Hwy. Hwy. 395

To Los Angeles

SIERRA NEVADA

CONTENTS

Beavertail cactus

Cottontop cactus

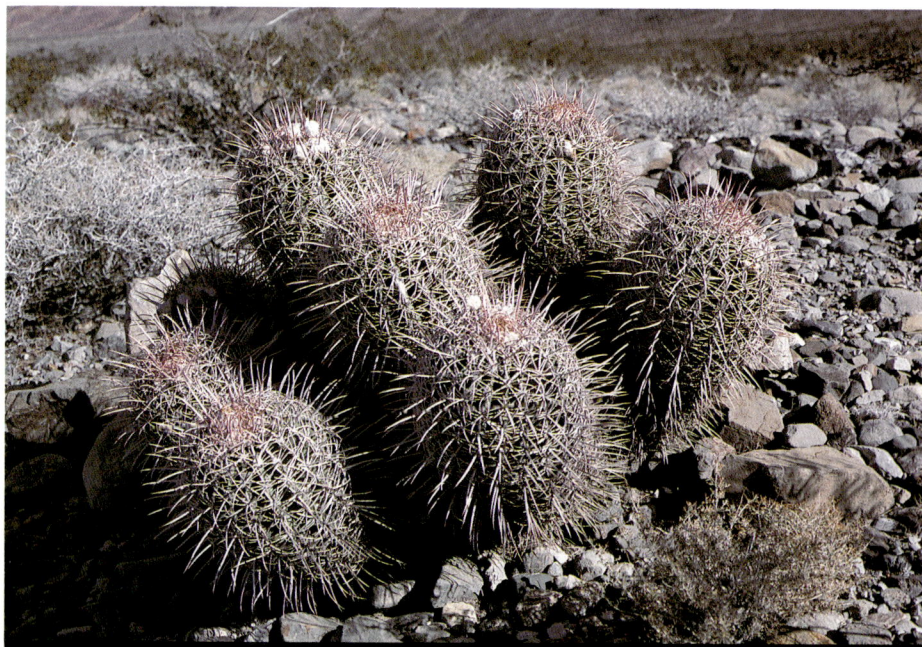

PREFACE

Welcome to Death Valley National Park. This book is designed to guide visitors on a driving tour of the major sights in this spectacular land of shimmering deserts, snow-covered mountains, and immense vistas of everchanging light and color. It is planned for the reader who has about two days for a visit, with the first day a tour of scenic points within 27 miles of Furnace Creek including Zabriskie Point, Dante's View and Badwater. For the second day's trip we suggest a longer drive north from Furnace Creek, with visits to Scotty's Castle, Ubehebe Crater and the magnificent sand dunes near Stove Pipe Wells.

If you're lucky enough to be spending more time in this fascinating desert, you'll find some hiking trails listed on page 43. We don't include the many intriguing roads that are accessible only by 4-wheel drive vehicles, but some scenic gravel roads that are usually safe to explore with a passenger car are described on page 40.

Besides telling the geologic story of how this vast desert came to be, this book also describes something of Death Valley's climate, plants, wildlife and pioneer history. But space is limited and there is much more to be said; for those who have a special interest in any of these topics we include a list of suggested reading with more detailed information.

The trips for both Day 1 and Day 2 start from the Furnace Creek Visitor Center. In a few places we have recommended a short trip on a dirt road, but those we have marked with a special symbol. Such roads are well-maintained and suitable for a passenger car, but if driving on gravel makes you nervous or if there has been a sudden rainstorm you might want to pass

Zabriskie Point

them by. The following symbols in the text indicate major points of interest:

 Stop in the parking area, climb out of the car and look around.

 Stop in the parking area and take the suggested short walk.

 Things to notice from the car while driving between stops.

 Graded dirt road; watch for muddy spots or dust clouds.

The number following the symbol shows the total miles driven. For example, (6.1) means that your mileage indicator should show that it is 6.1 miles since you started your guided tour.

If you are visiting Death Valley in summer, special caution is advised because of the extreme heat. Check at the Visitor Center for a leaflet called Hot Weather Hints with tips for summertime desert safety. If you're visiting in the middle of winter, remember that daylight hours are short; the sun drops behind the Panamints before 4 PM, so try to start your sightseeing early.

INTRODUCTION

Most of the Earth's valleys have been carved by streams, but Death Valley is an exception. Its deep floor reaches 282 feet below sea level and the streams that dry up in its sink are filling the valley with sediments, not wearing it deeper. The rugged mountain ranges that flank Death Valley rise one to two miles above the valley floor, and the huge fans of gravel at the foot of these ranges are dramatic evidence that the valley has been and still is being filled with broken rock.

Death Valley is scarred by erosion, but the principal architects of its shape and size are the forces that are arching and pulling apart this region of California. Earthquakes, rare but large, push the Black Mountains higher, drop the valley, and tilt the Panamint Range.

Geologists call this landscape "basin and range" country. Large segments of the Earth's crust are slowly stretching apart and tilting; their upturned edges are the mountain ranges, the downdropped edges — filled with sediments — are the valleys. Basin and range country extends from the Sierra of California across Nevada to central Utah. Near Badwater in Death Valley is the lowest point in the western hemisphere; Mount Whitney on the Sierra crest, only 85 miles and three ranges to the west, is the highest place in the 48 states. Basin and range country is rough, rugged, yet beautiful; harsh but true.

Scant soil or vegetation hides the rocks, sand, and salt flats of Death Valley. William Manly, who was one of the pioneers lost in the valley in 1849, noted that "...pretty near all creation was in sight..." Earth scientists today would agree with that description.

WEST

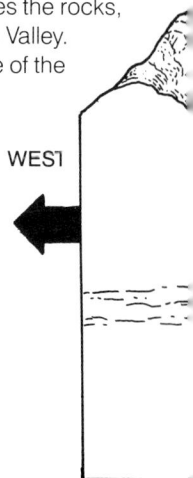

The rocky ribs of Death Valley tell geological stories that began nearly 2 billion years ago. At least 4 generations of rocks are exposed in the surrounding mountains, and that is where these stories are recorded. The earliest rocks are hard and complex, tortured by heat and pressure in the core of an ancient mountain system. Covering them are layers of marine sediments that have been hardened by time and squeezed into folds. During the crumpling of these layers, large masses of molten rock rose from depth and slowly cooled to form coarsely crystalline granites. Still later, these new mountains were broken by uplift and extension, and conditions became more like those in Death Valley today. Lake sediments, gravel deposits from torrential streams, and volcanic flows and ashes formed the rock sequences upturned in the colorful hills that now border the valley. You will see many telltale rocks and landscapes as you tour Death Valley. No one knows its whole story — there is always more to be discovered.

The chief characteristics of a desert are heat, aridity and barrenness; Death Valley is infamous for all three. Its record high temperature of 134 °F, measured in 1913, has been exceeded only once (in Libya), and its mean summer readings are the highest anywhere on Earth. As for aridity, in an average year only 1.9 inches of rain fall while the potential evaporation rate is 100 times that amount; that's dry. The vast playas below sea level — too salty to support any plant life — stretch so far they seem to have no limit.

Deserts occur in wide belts around the Earth where atmospheric circulation favors descending air masses. They also form on the leeward side of high mountain ranges in so-called "rain shadows". Death Valley is at the edge of the Northern Hemisphere's desert belt, and downwind of the Sierra Nevada and Panamint Ranges. These factors, combined with its low elevation, make it dry year-round and torrid in summer.

But the image of Death Valley as a lifeless inferno is a false one. The National

Stretching of the Earth's crust forms Death Valley
Adapted from Laura Serpa and others

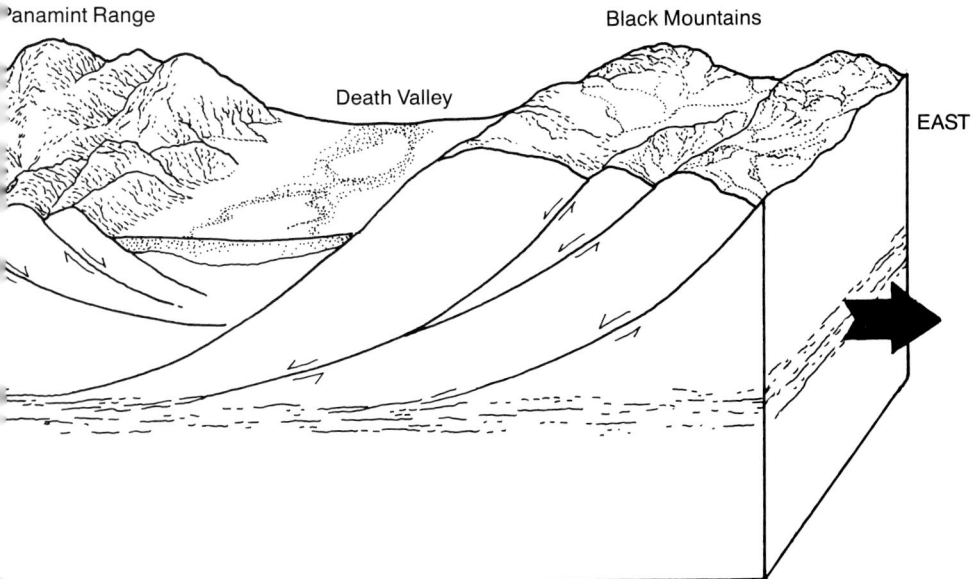

Panamint Range

Black Mountains

Death Valley

EAST

7

Furnace Creek Inn

Dante's View

Park as a whole has a great variety of flora and fauna, some with amazing stories of adaptation. With elevations ranging from below sea level to over 11,000 feet, 4 major life zones are encompassed — the Lower Sonoran from the valley floor to 4,000 feet; the Upper Sonoran to about 8,500 feet; then a narrow transition zone, and above 9,000 feet the Sub-Alpine. Every rise in elevation means increasing rainfall and cooler temperatures, so a wide range of animals and plants find suitable habitat.

Since long before history began, humans have made Death Valley their home. Artifacts have been found from Indian villages inhabited as much as 9,000 years ago, when the climate was more benign than it is today. Even as the climate became more harsh other groups of Indians moved in and out of Death Valley over thousands of years, with the Shoshone — some of whom still winter here — arriving about 1,000 years ago.

The long cycles of human history in Death Valley changed forever in 1849 when a band of emigrants took a misguided shortcut on their way to the California gold fields and stumbled down Furnace Creek Wash into the valley. Their story of survival and escape was harrowing, but it did not deter the wave of gold seekers who had heard fabulous tales of rich strikes and lost mines. Starting in 1850 Death Valley was home to prospectors and promoters, boom towns and ghost towns in a frenzy that lasted into the 1920's. Borax was one of Death Valley's few success stories, with mining profitable until recent years.

Death Valley is one of America's largest, most varied, and starkly beautiful National Parks. Start your tour, and see its wonders for yourself.

SOUTH FROM FURNACE CREEK

Furnace Creek is the starting point for both the first and second day's tours in this road guide. This desert oasis is watered by the diverted flow from Travertine and Texas Springs, warm springs near the mouth of Furnace Creek Canyon. Springs are central to desert life, and these near Furnace Creek have always played an important role in the history of Death Valley. A winter village of Shoshone Indians was located here for many centuries, and some of the California gold seekers who lost their way west in 1849 were saved by these copious springs that flow more than 1,000 gallons a minute.

Their source is mysterious, though the minerals dissolved in the water indicate that it has trickled underground for many miles from south-central Nevada. Some of its dissolved load of calcium carbonate is precipitated into layers of travertine rock where the springs discharge. Much of the water stays underground, percolating slowly down into the valley beneath the loose rocks and sand of Furnace Creek Fan. Despite the popular notion that Furnace Creek was named for its warm springs and desert heat, the name actually came from a small smelting furnace that was built near the mouth of the canyon by early gold and silver prospectors.

Today Furnace Creek is still the center of life in Death Valley. The National Park Headquarters, Furnace Creek Ranch, Furnace Creek Inn, and the main campgrounds are located here. Its 1,800 date palms planted in the 1920's and thousands of tamarisk trees, invaders brought in for windbreaks, provide welcome, cooling shade. You don't have to visit the Sahara Desert to see an oasis; Furnace Creek is a thriving example.

Hiking in Death Valley's canyons

Zabriskie Point

Alluvial fan

Artist's Palette

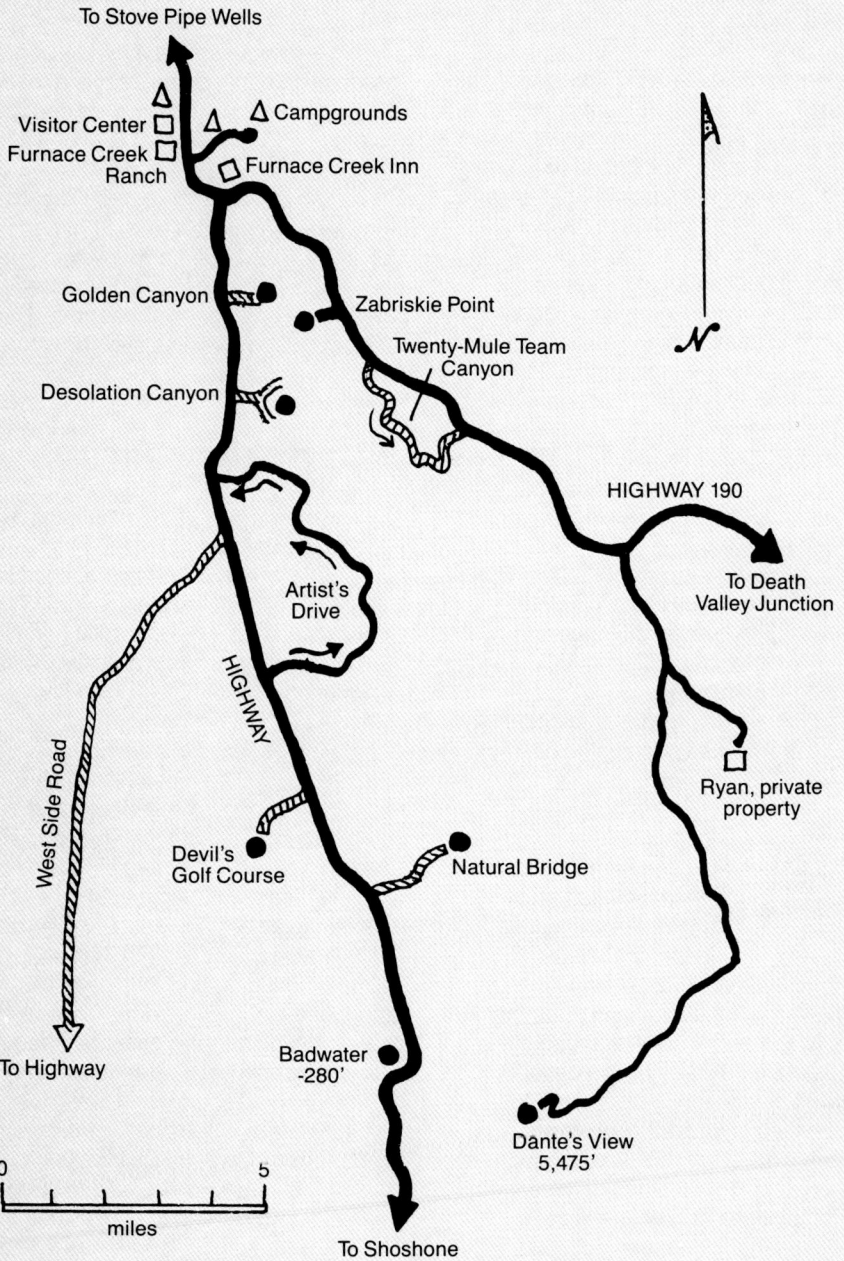

To Stove Pipe Wells

Visitor Center
Furnace Creek Ranch
Campgrounds
Furnace Creek Inn

Golden Canyon
Zabriskie Point
Twenty-Mule Team Canyon

Desolation Canyon

HIGHWAY 190

Artist's Drive

To Death Valley Junction

West Side Road

HIGHWAY

Ryan, private property

Devil's Golf Course
Natural Bridge

To Highway

Badwater -280'

0   5
miles

Dante's View 5,475'

To Shoshone

SOUTH FROM FURNACE CREEK

Furnace Creek Visitor Center

(0.0) Take some time to browse in the museum and book shop, and be sure to pick up a copy of the Death Valley map and brochure issued by the National Park Service. Exhibits in the museum include Death Valley's history as well as its geologic story, and information about prehistoric human cultures, climate, plants and animals, and borax mining. The topographic model provides a fine birds-eye view of the valley and the mountains that surround it. Have a look for Dante's View, Furnace Creek, and Badwater, to get some perspective on today's tour.

When you are ready to start exploring make sure your car is full of gas and carry some drinking water. Set your trip meter to zero or note your mileage indicator. As you leave the parking area turn right on the main road and head south; the next stop will be in 4.8 miles.

At (1.0) miles you can see Furnace Creek Inn on your left at the mouth of Furnace Creek Canyon. Built in the late 1920's by the Pacific Coast Borax Company to accommodate the increasing number of visitors, this luxury hotel changed the image of Death Valley from a desolate inferno to a stylish winter resort. Beautifully constructed of colorful local stone including travertine that was deposited by earlier generations of the nearby springs, the wings of the Inn enclose a palm garden with clear, bubbling streams and ponds that would delight Omar Khayyam.

At (1.3) miles a road to the right turns off to Badwater; continue straight ahead into the canyon of Furnace Creek. These intermittent desert stream beds are often called "dry washes", but the name does not always fit. In 1950, a summer thunderstorm poured a flood 8-feet deep down this wash, ripping away the road in some places, burying it in mud and gravel in others.

Here and there along Furnace Creek Wash you will see a few date palms growing where ground water exists just below the surface of the dry stream bed. Birds have carried the seeds, spreading the palms from the plantation at Furnace Creek Ranch.

Zabriskie Point

(4.8) Turn right into the parking lot and walk up the short trail to the overlook. The landscape here, though starkly beautiful, is called badlands because of its barren, rugged appearance.

The soft rock layers that surround Zabriskie Point were deposited in an earlier generation of mountain lake basin that was similar in some ways to the present valley but that had a wetter climate. The oldest sediments here accumulated as mud, sand, and gravel in and around a major lake. The gravel formed in washes and fans near the mountain borders as it does today, the sand on beaches and bars near the lakeshore, and the mud settled to the bottom of the still water in deeper parts of the lake. The lighter colors — yellows, tans, and browns — are mostly from iron minerals exposed to air; the darker ones — gray-green to dark gray — are volcanic ash and lava flows.

During a time span from about 9 to 3 million years ago, when these sedimentary rocks and their capping lava flows were accumulating, camels, mastodons, and

Devil's Golf Course

Badwater

Salt flats

big cats left some tracks and bones behind. These are scarce and you probably won't see any, but such rare finds help geologists establish the age and environment in which these rock layers formed.

Sometimes in long dry periods the lakes evaporated into layers of salty mud. Over many centuries the basin in which these rocks were being deposited, and the climate of the area, were becoming more and more like today's Death Valley. As the present valley continues to stretch and sink, some of these older rocks are heaved and twisted upward and exposed to a new cycle of erosion by rains, flooding streams, and wind. Geologic evolution is continually creating new sediments, structures, and landscapes as it destroys its older creations.

One intriguing aspect of badland erosion is the way in which its appearance is repeated at several scales. Look at the pattern of the hills and valleys at a scale of a few miles, and then look at the furrows on the side of a single hill covering a few hundred feet. In many ways they are the same. Even a close up photograph of a few square feet of soft, eroding badland sediments will look much the same as the overview of the strange colorful landscape that surrounds Zabriskie Point.

People have left few marks here, only some names. Manly Beacon, the high pinnacle of badlands between here and the valley, was named for William Manly, one of the pioneers who wandered into Death Valley in 1849. The point was named for Christian Zabriskie, for many years the general manager of the Pacific Coast Borax Company.

Turn right on the main road after leaving the parking lot; the next stop will be in 11.7 miles.

Twenty-Mule Team Canyon

(6.3) (Trailers are not permitted on this road.) Turn right onto a one-way dirt road that rejoins the highway in 2.9 miles. This road leads through Twenty-Mule Team Canyon, with close-up views of the colorful rock layers and badlands seen from Zabriskie Point. Here and there you'll see a prospector's tunnel driven into the soft, still-eroding rocks. These prospects were for borax, not gold or silver. Do not enter tunnels; they may be dangerous.

Some borax minerals were formed by evaporation in these older lake sediments, but they were mixed with mud and were too low grade to mine. However, as the later volcanic rocks in these layers were erupted, hot-spring waters percolating through the sediments redissolved the borax. Cooling and mixing along their underground courses, these thermal waters deposited high-grade lodes of borax minerals. Such concentrated deposits lured prospectors to these barren hills.

Vegetation is almost non-existent in these badlands. Several factors probably combine to cause this moonscape appearance: rainfall is low, and what little rain does fall mainly runs off instead of soaking in. Added to that the high salt content in the dry, loosely cemented layers of mud, and ongoing erosion that prevents soil from forming, effectively keep most plants from getting a foothold.

Where Twenty-Mule Team Canyon Road rejoins the main road, turn right. If you stayed on the highway instead of driving this scenic dirt road, subtract 1.3 from the mileages beyond here.

(11.5) The glossy green plants that dot the landscape in this area are creosote bush, probably the most common shrub in Death Valley at this elevation. It grows about head high, and has roots that can spread out to 50 feet. Notice how the bushes seem to be spaced in regular intervals, as if in a giant orchard. This is because the roots of the creosote bush give off a poison that kills any seedlings (including its own) that try to come up near it. This prevents overcrowding, and ensures that the "mother" plant will have no competition for the sparse rain that falls in its vicinity. The shrub has a distinct odor that resembles creosote, hence its name.

At (13.4) turn right on the road to Dante's View. The mine dumps and buildings you see in the next few miles are the remains of extensive borax mining operations that continued here until 1986. The Ryan and Billie Mines are in mothballs now, but if the price of borax should increase sufficiently, mining would probably begin again. These mines are on private property, and trespassing is prohibited.

Desert Varnish

(16.5) There is no specific turnout here, but for several hundred yards the road shoulder is wide enough for you to park. If you walk to your right onto the rocky ground, you'll notice that most of the rocks glitter in the sunshine. They are dark brown to nearly black, and look as if they had been shellacked. This is a natural rock weathering product called desert varnish, a tough, thin layer of iron and manganese oxides and clay minerals. It takes thousands of years for a layer of desert varnish to accumulate, and in some cases it can be used to estimate the length of time that rock surfaces have been

exposed. Have a look, but don't break or collect nature's varnished rocks.

The next stop will be in 10 miles. If you are pulling a trailer, plan to leave it in the trailer parking lot 4.5 miles ahead; beyond 9.5 miles the road is so steep that trailers are not allowed.

As you pass the trailer parking lot on the right at (21) miles, notice how the road points straight ahead up the alluvial fan. This inclined surface is an apron of gravel and sand that has been washed down from the Black Mountains by flash floods over thousands of years. The transition of the smooth slope into steeper, more rugged topography marks the upper edge of the alluvial fan. This is the change from erosional deposits of the fan to bedrock. As the road crosses this transition it begins to zigzag up a shallow canyon in the bedrock of the Black Mountains.

Dante's View

(26.6) The superb views from here give some sense of the immensity of Death Valley and its mountain walls. The elevation at Dante's View is 5,475 feet. Badwater, the white salt flat directly below, is 280 feet below sea level, and Telescope Peak, the high point of the great Panamint Range across the valley soars to 11,049 feet. From here you can look a mile down to the valley floor and a mile up to the next mountain range west. Telescope Peak is 21 miles away in a straight line, and the valley floor is 5 miles across. Although you can't see it all from here, Death Valley is more than 100 miles long. Five hundred-fifty square miles of it are below sea level, and it is still sinking.

The salt, mud and coarser sediments that fill the valley are estimated to be as much

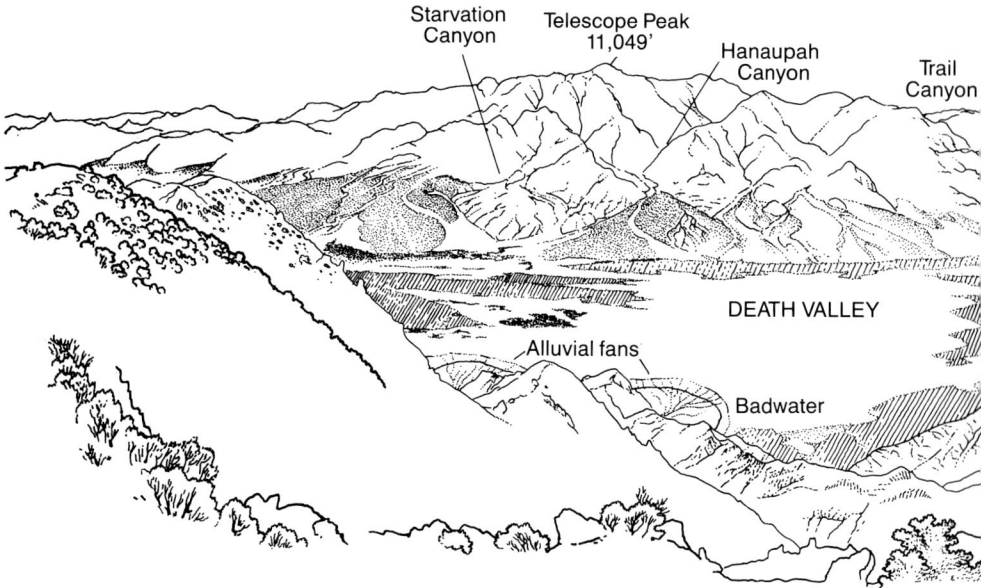

PANAMINT RANGE

Starvation Canyon — Telescope Peak 11,049' — Hanaupah Canyon — Trail Canyon — DEATH VALLEY — Alluvial fans — Badwater

as 15,000 feet thick. Since the present valley is about 3 million years old, the rate of sinking must be only about 6 inches every hundred years, and that rate is probably not continuous. It is more likely that much of the sinking occurs in sudden earthquakes — every few hundred years — when the valley drops several feet along the faults that border its eastern side.

Geologists call this type of structural valley a graben, the German word for grave. Think of a wall of loose blocks slowly slumping apart; a keystone-shaped block will drop as the blocks on either side move apart. The zone of slippage between the blocks is called a fault. In many structural valleys, one side sinks more than the other, and this is the case in Death Valley. In fact, the steep slope between here and Badwater is the eroded face of one of the fault zones on which the valley is sinking and tilting toward the east.

Across the valley at the base of the Panamint Range are several excellent examples of alluvial fans — boulders,

gravel, sand and clay washed down from the eroding mountains. The largest floods carry the big boulders, smaller ones the gravel and sand, and even trickles of water can keep the mud particles and dissolved rock chemicals moving down to the valley. In this way the sediments are roughly sorted, leaving boulders and gravel on the fans and sweeping the mud and salts onto the valley floor. As the fans from each canyon merge toward the valley they form a nearly continuous apron of alluvial (which means washed) debris. A common feature in the desert southwest, Spanish explorers named these alluvial aprons "bajadas", a word that means slopes.

Spanish words are common in this region. The name for the salt and mud flats of dried up lake beds is playa (a Spanish word that also means beach). The white and tan area in the valley bottom below Dante's View is a playa; the sink of the Amargosa River that flows in from the south, Salt Creek from the north, and the side canyons from the mountains east and west of the valley floor. When rainfall has

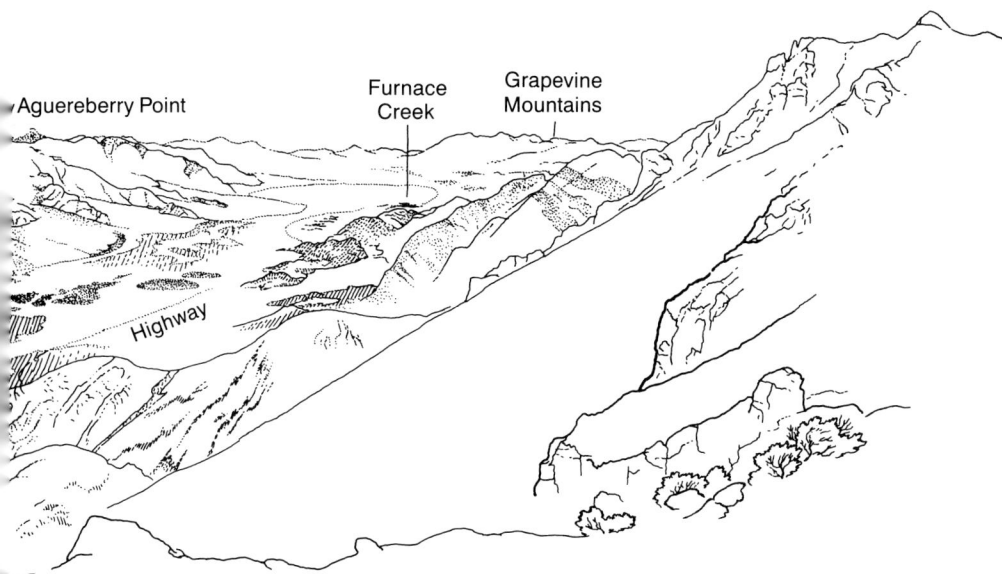

Aguereberry Point — Furnace Creek — Grapevine Mountains — Highway

PANORAMA FROM DANTE'S VIEW

been above normal, parts of the playa are covered by standing water. In dryer years, evaporating salt layers paint some of the once-tan mud flats a blinding white.

Down on the valley floor the temperature is about 25 °F higher than here at Dante's View. As wind stirs the air, some of it rises and cools while other air masses descend and become warmer. The heat content in the air stays about the same, but air expands as it rises and its heat is diluted to fill the larger volume. The reverse occurs as air descends and compresses. A handy rule in mountain country is that about 5 °F of cooling occurs with every 1,000 feet of elevation.

Rainfall is low and evaporation high on the valley floor, while in the mountains rain increases and can turn to snow at higher elevations. These rapid changes in temperature and moisture create several climate zones in Death Valley and its surrounding mountain ranges. The Bristlecone pines on Telescope Peak are among the world's oldest living trees, but

they would die in a few days in the hot weather and brackish ground water at the edges of the playa. In turn, the pickleweed that thrives there would die in one bitter cold night on the high ridges of the Panamint Range. Nature has its scheme of things.

But the essence of Nature is change. If you had been here 12,000 years ago, toward the close of the last great ice age, you would have looked down on a great lake — 90 miles long, 6 to 11 miles wide, and 600 feet deep. The overall climate was cooler and wetter, and water flowed all year in the streams. Huge volumes of melt water from vast snow and ice fields that covered the Sierra Nevada poured down into a chain of lakes in what is now Owens Valley and the Mojave region. Lake Manly in Death Valley was the last lake in the chain; the water stopped here.

The ice ages have waxed and waned over the past 2 million years, a total of perhaps 20 cycles of cold and warm climate. Did Lake Manly fill and evaporate many times?

19

Life Zones of Death Valley Region

Bristlecone & limber pines — SUB-ALPINE ZONE

Pinyon pine — UPPER SONORAN ZONE

Desert holly Creosote bush

Saltbush Mesquite Pickleweed — LOWER SONORAN ZONE

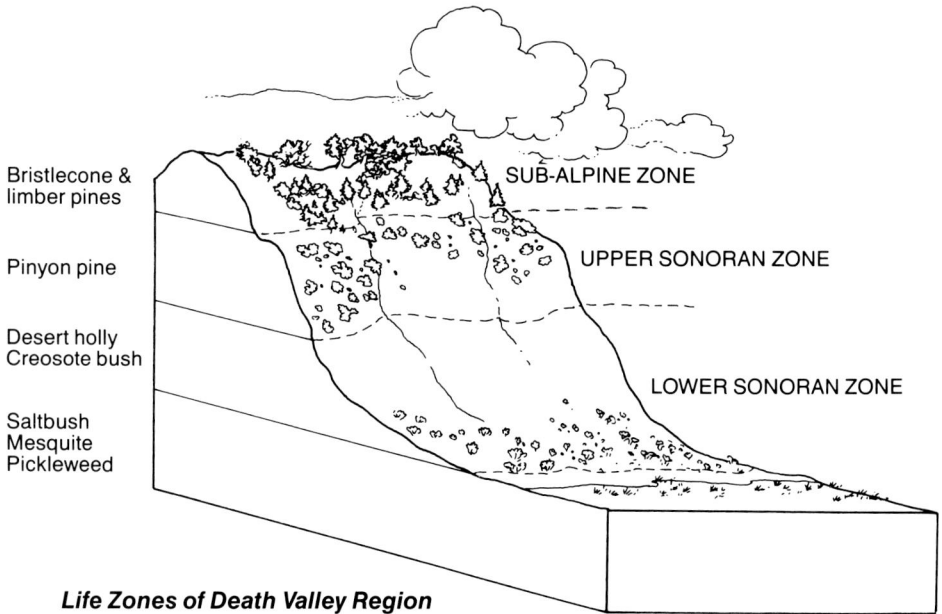

The answer is probably yes, but each generation of geologic change destroys some of the clues like ancient shoreline scars that document the last time a great lake filled Death Valley.

The next stop will be in 25 miles back at Furnace Creek, but there are still many things to see during the return trip.

As you leave Dante's View look out over the landscape to the east, away from Death Valley; it is an excellent example of basin and range topography. The Greenwater Range is about 7 miles away; behind that is Resting Spring Range, about 30 miles distant on the California-Nevada border. The high peaks in the distance are the Spring Mountains, about 60 miles away; Charleston Peak, the crest, is 11,918 feet high, and Las Vegas is in the basin just beyond it.

While driving down the straight road on the alluvial fan, notice that the Greenwater Range across the valley is a mesa capped with dark lava flows. The white scars on top of the mesa are sites where boreholes were drilled down into the sediments beneath the lava by companies exploring for borax.

To the left and beyond the Greenwater Range, distinct layers of tilted and folded rocks are clearly exposed in the Funeral Mountains. These rocks — limestones, dolomites, quartzites and shales — were deposited in a shallow ocean 700 to 300 million years ago, and were compressed into folds before being uplifted and tilted. Geologic time has played the Death Valley region like an accordian, alternately squeezing and stretching the area into folds and faults. The great forces have changed over the eons, but the bent and broken rocks record their passing and their sequence. Geologic time is immense; the fact that the oldest rocks in the Death Valley region were formed nearly 2 billion years ago is almost incomprehensible. Here is a thought experiment that may help in understanding such a vastness of time: if 2 billion years were compressed into one year, the average person's lifetime by comparison would be 1 second.

On a more human time scale, reflect as you drive down Furnace Creek Wash that it was less than 150 years ago when the first group of pioneers led their ox teams and wagons into Death Valley by this same route.

The second part of today's tour will begin again at Furnace Creek.

Furnace Creek Visitor Center

(0.0) Drive south from Furnace Creek, and at (1.3) miles, near Furnace Creek Inn, turn right on the road to Badwater. This junction is near the top of the Furnace Creek fan, one of the largest alluvial fans on the east side of Death Valley. As you drive down the fan, notice how rapidly the vegetation changes. On the high part of the fan it is a long way down to ground water, so vegetation is sparse and made up of plants like desert holly (see photo on back cover) that need very little water. Farther down, at (2.6) miles, darker green mesquite trees are the dominant plants. They need fresh ground water, but can put roots down more than fifty feet to reach it.

Toward the lower edge of Furnace Creek fan, the fresh ground water beneath the surface begins to mingle with the saline ground water of the playa. In this zone of shallow brackish ground water, pickleweed is the most common plant. Beyond the base of the fan are the white salt flats, with such high salinity that all vegetation disappears.

Golden Canyon

(3.3) Turn left into the Golden Canyon parking lot. The hike into the canyon is a 1 1/2 mile round trip up an easy grade. A trail guide booklet is available at Furnace Creek Visitor Center, and usually from a box at the trailhead.

Golden Canyon is named for the glowing color of the canyon walls; the views up the canyon of the yellow rocks against a deep blue sky are spectacular. These rocks are the same older playa and lake sediments seen from Zabriskie Point. The layers were originally horizontal, but have been tilted 45° or more.

Stream erosion in a desert canyon like this one is a sporadic process. Some years almost no rain falls in Death Valley; other years bring cloudbursts that dump an inch

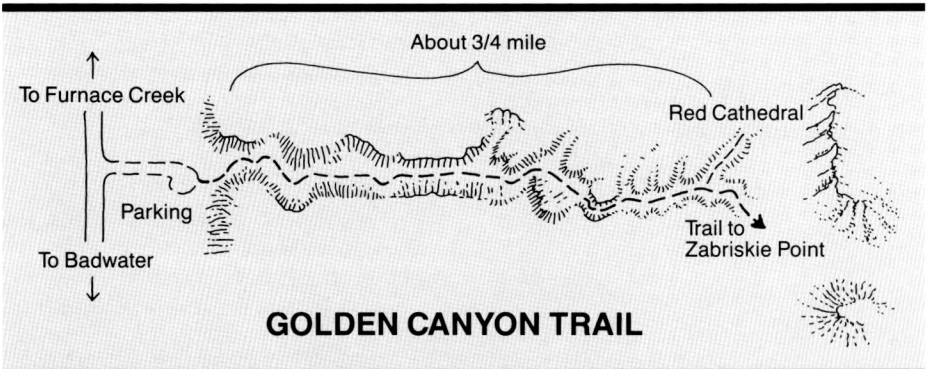

About 3/4 mile

To Furnace Creek

Red Cathedral

Parking

Trail to
Zabriskie Point

To Badwater

GOLDEN CANYON TRAIL

or more in a few hours. A flash flood can quickly abrade a foot or more down into these soft sediments. A paved road once led up into Golden Canyon, but was washed out by a sudden storm in 1976. The few remnants of the road are convincing evidence of the power of flowing water.

After hiking up Golden Canyon for about half an hour, return by the same trail. If you have time for a longer hike, a colorful formation called Red Cathedral can be seen farther up the canyon. Near Red Cathedral a side trail continues 2 miles more to Zabriskie Point. From the Golden Canyon parking lot turn left on the highway; the next stop is in 10.2 miles.

 When you have driven about a mile past Golden Canyon you will find yourself surrounded by the legendary emptiness of Death Valley. The bare hills on the left are the same rocks seen at Zabriskie Point and in Golden Canyon, and the white salt flats to the right seem devoid of life. However,

much of the Death Valley lore and its sometimes gruesome names were made up by prospectors and promoters who wanted to embellish its mysterious reputation. Relatively few people have died from the elements in Death Valley. Its landscapes are starkly beautiful, not lifeless; specialized communities of plants and animals thrive in the diverse environments in the valley and its surrounding mountains. When treated with respect, Death Valley is seldom deadly. At (7.3) miles pass by the turnoff of the West Side Road.

Devil's Golf Course

 (12.2) Turn right on the gravel road and drive down the fan onto the desert sink.

 The parking lot at (13.5) miles is surrounded by rough blocks of dusty, crystalline salt. Touch one of these jagged blocks to feel how

sharp the tiny crystals are. The rugged ground here is formed by salt — about 95% pure table salt — crystallizing and expanding. About 2,000 years ago a saline, 30-foot-deep lake temporarily covered this part of the playa. As the lake dried, the dissolved salt precipitated into a layer about 4 feet thick. Heat and cold, as well as solution by rains and recrystallization by drying, have caused the salt layer to expand and contract over the years, heaving it into this jumble. New salt crystals keep forming as the shallow saline ground water rises to the surface and evaporates. The new crystals are white; older crystals are covered with dust blown in from nearby mud flats.

Beneath the Devil's Golf Course lie thousands of feet of alternating layers of salt and lake sediments that accumulate as the valley sinks and the generations of lakes similar to Lake Manly come and go. Millions of years in the future these flat layers may be slowly uplifted on the flanks of yet another valley, to be eroded into badlands similar to those in Golden Canyon.

Return to the highway and turn right. If you elected not to take the gravel road to Devil's Golf Course, subtract 2.6 from the mileages beyond here.

Pass by the turnoff to Natural Bridge, and at about (20) miles you will see a square, white sign on the cliff ahead. This marks sea level; if the ocean could reach into Death Valley, you would be more than 250 feet under water. Theoretically if ocean water were piped into the valley electrical energy could be generated from its fall, and the high rate of evaporation — more than 10 feet of water a year — would give the scheme a long life. This is just a wild idea, but it does emphasize the low elevation, high temperature and aridity of this unusual desert basin. The Dead Sea

between Israel and Jordan is 1,312 feet below sea level, and the same scheme to generate power has been proposed seriously there.

Badwater

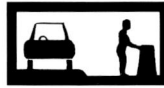

(20.3) The shallow pool below the parking lot is fed by water that rises along the eastern boundary fault of the valley. Containing mostly sodium chloride, it is saltier than the sea. One of the early surveyors who determined that this place is 280 feet below sea level saw that his mule wouldn't drink from the pool and noted "badwater" on his map. The name stuck. Though not poisonous, it is not drinkable.

But even here life persists. Larvae of insects can be seen wiggling in the water, and tiny water beetles live on patches of algae. A few clumps of pickleweed grow near the pond's edge. You can recognize it by its segmented green stems that look like tiny links of sausage. Water, bad though it may be, is the liquid of life.

Although Furnace Creek Ranch is well below sea level, Badwater is even lower, and a few miles to the west is the lowest spot in North America — minus 282 feet. Since temperature increases as elevation decreases, Badwater is one of the world's hottest places. Death Valley's record high temperature of 134°F was measured at Furnace Creek Ranch in 1913; the temperature at Badwater that day probably reached 135° or 136°F. For humans, whose normal body temperature is just below 99°F, that's hot.

This is the turn-around point for today, but before starting back notice the small alluvial fan just north of the parking lot. The colors of the rocks on the surface range from brown to gray, and these colors provide clues to the age of the gravel that

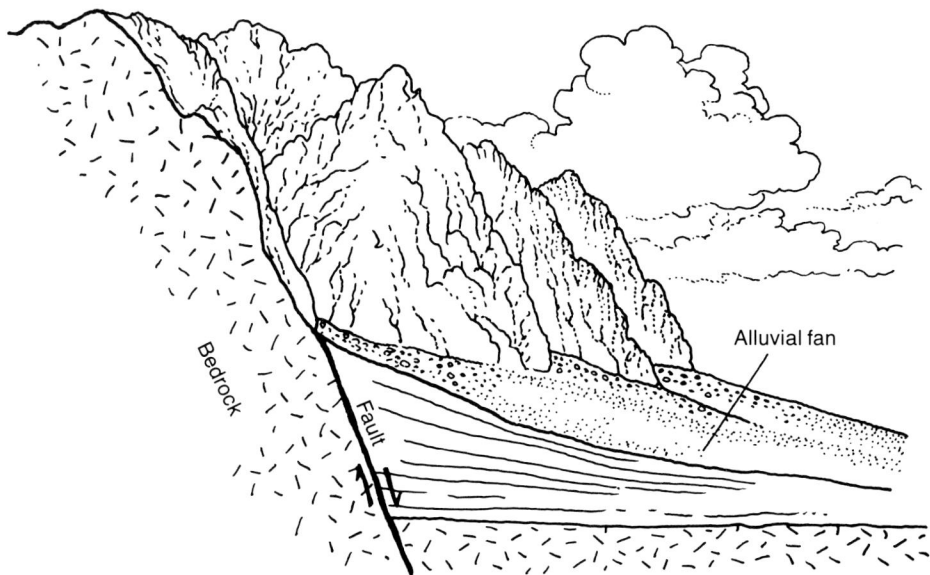

Alluvial fans form in desert regions at sides of down-dropped valleys

covers the fan. The darker brown is desert varnish that took thousands of years to form. The light gray areas are composed of younger rocks where desert varnish has not had time to develop. The bedrock of the Black Mountains is very old, nearly 2 billion years, but the pieces of rock were broken loose by erosion in the canyon relatively recently. The desert varnish started to form after the rocks were broken.

Here within a few hundred yards we can see three measures of geologic time: the bedrock of the mountain — 1.8 billion years old; the rock torn from the mountain and pounded by floods into the gravel that covers the alluvial fan — 10,000 to 10 years ago; and the white salt crystals that border the evaporating pond — perhaps they formed today. Mary Austin in her book THE LAND OF LITTLE RAIN says it much more poetically: "This is the sense of the desert hills, that there is room enough and time enough."

The next stop, on the way back toward Furnace Creek, will be in 12.6 miles.

Artist's Drive

(28.3) Turn right on this one-way road. Artist's Drive starts up a steep fan and winds through foothills composed of colorful sedimentary and volcanic rocks. Although these rocks are generally older than those at Zabriskie Point, their origins were similar — lake beds, alluvial fans, lava flows and volcanic ash deposits. The road crosses several steep, dry washes as it follows along the mountain front. Turn right at (32.6) miles into the parking area.

Artist's Palette

(32.9) Although the bright colors splashed across the hillsides here look like the work of a giant with a paintbrush, they were all painted by nature. The red, pink, yellow, orange and brown colors result mainly from two minerals that commonly occur in rust — hematite, a red iron oxide, and limonite, a yellow iron oxide. Other colors, especially the violets and greens, are formed by the alteration of minerals found in the volcanic ash.

Natural pigments made by grinding up colorful rocks such as these were used for paints by prehistoric people. Many of the pigments in today's paints and dyes are organic chemicals, which though bright and varied in color fade with time. Inorganic pigments like the ones in these rocks are much more permanent.

After leaving Artist's Palette the one-way road twists and turns through low, narrow canyons cut into old alluvial fan deposits. The layers of cemented gravel, called conglomerates, have been tilted by the slow upheaval of the Black Mountains. The beds exposed in these canyon walls give you a look at the inside of a typical alluvial fan.

If your timing has been fortunate, you'll return to the highway as the sun is setting behind the Panamint Range across the valley. The beauty of the dark mountain profile against a desert sky radiant with slowly deepening colors belies the morbid reputation of Death Valley. Turn right on the highway. The next stop will be 0.3 mile from this intersection.

Mushroom Rock

(37.8) Turn right into the parking area. The dark, hard rocks exposed here are basaltic lavas that have been polished smooth by the wind. Since most blowing sand moves in a turbulent air layer near the ground surface, the polishing action of wind erosion is most effective within several inches of the ground. The stem of mushroom rock will eventually be worn away by the intermittent sandblasting of desert windstorms. For hard rocks like basalt, this may take thousands of years; a wooden telephone pole whose base is not protected by a pile of rocks can be cut down by wind erosion in just a few years.

This is the last stop on today's tour. If you are staying in the Furnace Creek area, you may wish to see if there is a ranger program scheduled at the Visitor Center tonight.

DEATH VALLEY EXTREMES

Hottest temperature: 134°F (56.7°C), July 10, 1913

Coldest temperature: 15°F (-9.4°C), January 8, 1913

Driest years: no rainfall, 1929 and 1953

Wettest year: 4.60 inches (11.68 centimeters), 1941

Lowest point: -282 feet (-86 meters), west of Badwater

Highest point: 11,049 feet (3,368 meters), Telescope Peak

Oldest rocks: 1.8 billion years

Youngest rocks: salt crystals, still forming

NORTH FROM FURNACE CREEK

Death Valley National Park is immense. At 5,210 square miles, it is larger than the state of Connecticut. Death Valley itself is more than 100 miles long and about 5 to 10 miles wide, but the park includes huge mountain ranges and basins on both sides. Scotty's Castle and Ubehebe Crater, stops on today's tour, are 50 miles north of Furnace Creek. Fill your car with gas, and again set your trip meter to zero at Furnace Creek Visitor Center. As you leave the parking area turn north; the first stop will be in 1.7 miles.

Harmony Borax Works

(1.7) Turn left into the parking area. In this old ghost town are adobe buildings and remains of the borax processing plant.

Borax was discovered in the valley in 1873, but mining did not begin until the 1880's. Borate compounds in the saline water beneath the playa sometimes recrystallize at the surface of the salt pan into fibrous clusters called cottonballs. This mineral was raked into piles out on the salt pan by Chinese laborers, and brought to Harmony Borax works to be purified. Between 1883 and 1889, refined borax was hauled by the famous twenty-mule team wagons from here to the train station at Mojave — a distance of 165 miles.

More extensive deposits of borax were discovered in 1882 in older playa and vein deposits in the mountains east of Death Valley, but because of their inaccessibility large-scale mining of these deposits did not begin until 1907. Though borax is most familiar as a laundry detergent, its largest use is as a flux in lowering the melting temperature of glass and porcelain enamel. Its various compounds find such

diverse markets as an additive to gasoline and as a fire retardant. More information on borax is available in the interesting Borax Museum at Furnace Creek Ranch.

Borax does not have the glamour of gold, but more than $30,000,000 worth of the white powder had been produced from the Death Valley region by 1927. When the rich deposit of borate minerals at Boron in the Mojave Desert began production that year, Death Valley entrepreneurs switched from borax to tourism. As more and more visitors were drawn to Death Valley by its wild beauty and its unique natural features, it became evident that the desert was really a fragile environment and needed some protection from its admirers. To that end, Death Valley National Monument was created in 1933. In 1994 the monument was upgraded to a National Park and nearly 2,000 square miles were added to its size. The ghosts in this town were probably pleased. The next stop will be in 14.3 miles.

Mustard Canyon

(1.7) Leaving the borax works, turn left on a short, one-way dirt road that loops back to the highway through Mustard Canyon. The soft rock walls in this canyon are older playa deposits from the same rock sequence seen at Zabriskie Point, consisting of mud cemented by salt minerals. The canyon walls are usually mustard yellow in color, but after periods of higher than normal rainfall the dampness evaporating from the more porous rocks can deposit a crust of white salt crystals that looks like snow.

At (2.9) miles turn left onto the highway. If you did not take the Mustard Canyon road, subtract 0.4 from mileages beyond here.

(6.0) For the next few miles the highway crosses the lower slopes of several alluvial fans. The rocky ground supports a sparse cover of creosote bush, desert holly, and turtleback — a sprawling bush whose shape prompted its name. Some fans are covered almost exclusively with either creosote bush or desert holly, while others have a mixture of species. Why some fans support many types of plants and others are covered mostly by one species is not fully understood. It probably has to do with the character of the lean, rocky soil developed on each fan, which in

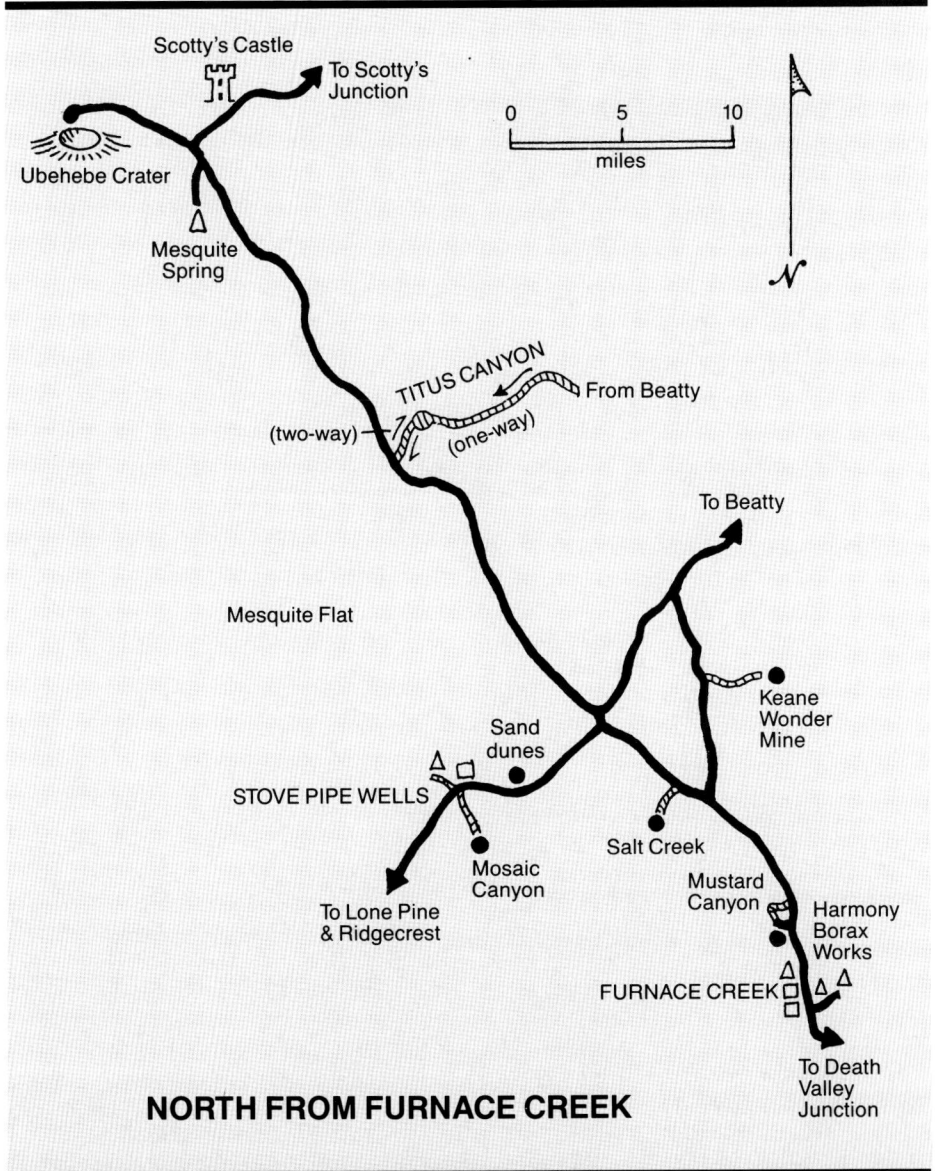

Scotty's Castle

To Scotty's Junction

Ubehebe Crater

Mesquite Spring

0   5   10
miles

TITUS CANYON

From Beatty

(two-way)   (one-way)

To Beatty

Mesquite Flat

Keane Wonder Mine

Sand dunes

STOVE PIPE WELLS

Salt Creek

Mustard Canyon

Harmony Borax Works

Mosaic Canyon

To Lone Pine & Ridgecrest

FURNACE CREEK

To Death Valley Junction

NORTH FROM FURNACE CREEK

Registered trademark of
United States Borax & Chemical Corporation

TWENTY-MULE TEAMS

From 1883 to 1889, ten thousand tons of borax were hauled out of Death Valley in great wagons. Each team pulled 2 wagons and a water tank that together weighed more than 36 tons. The haul to the railroad at Mojave was a round trip of 330 miles and took 20 days. In 100 YEARS OF U.S. BORAX, 1872-1972, a book published by United States Borax & Chemical Corporation, the teams' unique abilities are described:

"The famous twenty-mule teams actually consisted of 18 mules and 2 horses, the latter used at the wheel positions because of their strength and obedience. The teams were controlled by a single jerk line fixed to the bit of the near (left) mule, the smartest animal in the team, and carried over 100 feet to the driver's hand through rings on the near mules' harness. The driver either sat on the perch on the lead wagon or rode the near wheelhorse.

To signal a left turn the driver gave the jerk line a steady pull; repeated light jerks signaled a right turn. The lead mule knew the signals and led the rest of the team in the indicated direction. When the train made a turn it was necessary for some of the mules to pull against the direction of the turn; otherwise the wagons would be pulled across the curve rather than around it. The fours, sixes and eights (numbering from the wheelhorse) were trained to jump over the chain that ran the length of the train and pull in a contrary direction to keep the wagons on the right track. Many mules knew their work so well that they would jump the chain and start pulling as soon as they saw the lead mule begin the turn, without a word from the driver. When the turn was completed the mules jumped back into position, one span after the other."

turn depends on the nature of the bedrock upstream. Very little rain — about 1.9 inches a year on average — falls here, so all these plants have widespread surface roots to gather water and leaves that retain moisture.

If the ocean could reach Death Valley, the water here would be 200 feet deep; if Lake Manly at its highest level still filled the valley, it would be 300 feet deeper than that.

At (10 to 11) miles, notice the great rampart across the valley to the left. It is Tucki Mountain, at the north end of the Panamint Range. The huge fans which spill from its rugged canyons merge to form a continuous bajada before reaching the valley floor.

The road to the right at (11.4) miles leads up out of the valley to Beatty, Nevada.

(13.9) Turn left on the level dirt road (2.5 miles round trip) to Salt Creek. In most places water moving south along Death Valley toward Badwater flows underground, but ahead is an uplift of older, less permeable

sediments that forces the water to the surface in a year-round stream.

Salt Creek

(15.1) A guidebook for the Salt Creek Nature Trail is usually available at the start of this delightful boardwalk trail that crisscrosses the stream for a half-mile round trip. Unique plants and fish have evolved along this isolated, salty stream as Lake Manly slowly dried away.

The desert pupfish was the only fish to survive the evaporation of the lake. Twenty thousand years ago populations of ancestral pupfish species, among other kinds of fish, thrived in great fresh water lakes in this part of the southwest. As the climate became more arid and the lakes began to shrink, the remaining pools, springs, and short stretches of running streams fragmented the ancestral populations. Isolated from one another, each population faced different selective pressures in its changing habitat, accounting for the varied forms we see today.

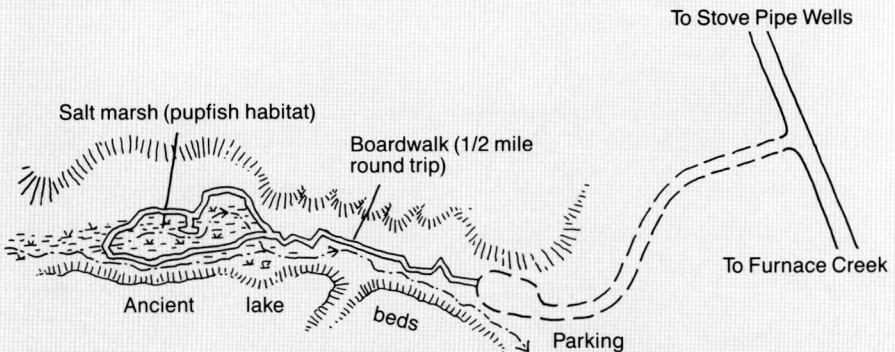

To Stove Pipe Wells

Salt marsh (pupfish habitat)

Boardwalk (1/2 mile round trip)

To Furnace Creek

Ancient   lake

beds

Parking

SALT CREEK NATURE TRAIL

Here at Salt Creek the water varies in temperature from near freezing to well over 100°F, and is as salty as the ocean. In a marsh farther south another species of pupfish survives in water 5 times saltier than sea water. The short life-cycle of pupfish — 3 to 4 generations per year — probably helped to speed their evolution. Also, they will eat almost anything; algae, insects, and if need be, each other.

Nine types of pupfish live in and near Death Valley, and a 10th has apparently become extinct. Is it really important that pupfish survive? Absolutely. Somewhere in their biochemistry is the secret of rapid adaptation, and in their vitality a symbol to admire.

Return to the highway and turn left. If you elected not to drive the gravel road to Salt Creek, subtract 2.4 from mileages beyond here. The next stop will be in 15.8 miles.

Pupfish

At (17.5) miles the highway reaches sea level. Looking ahead at the vast sweep of land, you can see that the northern half of Death Valley is offset to the west. The mountains that surround the valley change from the Panamints to the Cottonwoods on the west, and from the Funerals to the Grapevines on the east. In this offset, winds that sweep down or across the valley floor are forced to shift direction; in so doing they slow in velocity and drop the sand they have carried. The resulting sand dunes are visible ahead to the left. The last stop today will be a walk on these dunes.

At (20.3) turn right and continue up the valley to the northwest, toward Scotty's Castle. At (26.5) notice the rock formations ahead to the right. The soft, tan-to-reddish outcrops in the middleground are badlands similar to the rocks at Zabriskie Point, while the high, darker Grapevine Mountains in the background are composed of marine sediments that were

deposited 700 to 300 million years ago and cemented into hard rocks. Their sharp, rugged relief shows that the bedrock layers are hard and brittle, while the closer, rounded hills indicate softer and generally younger formations.

Alluvial Fans

(32.1) A display in the turnout explains more about fans. They come in many sizes and shapes; the smaller, steeper fans, such as the one here, are generally formed by steep canyons with small watershed areas. In larger canyons floods are bigger and more frequent, building larger, more gently sloping fans. A fan is something like an hour glass with debris from the mountains funneling through a narrow opening to spill out in the valley. However, canyon erosion and fan deposition takes centuries, not hours, and the tumbling down is intermittent instead of continuous.

If you haven't had a close-up view of desert holly, take a look at the bushes growing near this sign. You can see from the shape of their gray leaves why they have the name. In especially dry years, these plants take on an almost lavender cast. The next stop will be in 24.5 miles.

At (35.1) miles pass by the gravel road that turns right to Titus Canyon. This fascinating canyon is described on pages 40 and 43. If you are visiting Death Valley in early spring, and especially if there has been ample rainfall over the winter, you may be lucky enough to see the desert wildflowers in lavish bloom. If so, make some extra stops where the road shoulder is wide and firm, and walk a short way from the highway for a closer look at their delicate but tenacious beauty.

As you drive north keep an eye out for several kinds of cactus; they flourish above the 1,000 foot elevation. Don't expect to find the towering Saguaro and Organ Pipe cactus that are seen in Arizona; almost all Death Valley cacti are no more than knee high. The most common varieties are cottontop — clumps of fat barrels with white wooly tops; beavertail, with flat, spiny pads; and cholla — a branched cactus completely covered with wicked spines.

When in bloom they are all spectacular. Cottontop has yellow blooms, beavertail magenta, and cholla a greenish yellow. But even when they are not blooming they are worth a closer look — just be careful not to touch.

At (53) miles a road to the left leads to the camping and picnic area at Mesquite Spring, and there is a ranger station on the highway 0.5 mile beyond the campground turnoff. Just north of the entrance station turn right to Scotty's Castle.

Scotty's Castle

(56.6) Who was Scotty, and what is a Moorish castle doing in a remote Death Valley canyon? It's a long story and there is time to tell only part of it, but the tales of this valley and its most famous prospector, Death Valley Scotty, are inseparable.

Mark Twain defined a mine as a hole in the ground with a liar at the top. While that may come close to describing some of Scotty's promotions it is probably too harsh. He was a teller of tall tales, but a charming, fun-loving vagabond as well. He used other people's money, but paid them back in dreams.

Walter Scott headed west in the 1880's. More showman than cowboy, he travelled with Buffalo Bill's Wild West Show as a trick rider before taking up prospecting. Scotty's favorite game was finding wealthy backers for a "secret gold mine" in Death Valley. One of them, Albert Johnson, wanted to see the Death Valley mine in person, but after a couple of trips with Scotty he realized the mine was a grand illusion. On the first trip Scotty set up a fake ambush to prevent their reaching the mine. It was so realistic that Scotty's brother was shot, though fortunately not killed.

Johnson enjoyed his Death Valley trips with Scotty; the money he lost was apparently well spent on this new friend and spinner of dreams. Together they decided to build Johnson's vacation villa in the desert — Scotty's Castle. Johnson and Scotty were opposites: Johnson the quiet, practical businessman and Scotty the flamboyant promoter. With Scotty's dreams and Johnson's money and planning, they built this mansion during the 1920's. Johnson always kept a low profile, saying that it was Scotty's place and that he was only "Scotty's banker." Scotty always claimed the money came from his secret mine, and in a way it did.

In 1970, Death Valley Ranch — Scotty's Castle — was purchased by the National Park Service from the foundation to whom Johnson had willed it. Now it belongs to all of us.

One-hour guided tours of Scotty's Castle are scheduled from 9 AM to 5 PM every day. If there is a long wait for this very popular tour, you may wish to purchase tickets for later and drive on to see Ubehebe Crater first. In any case, plan to start back down the valley early enough to walk out on the sand dunes near Stove Pipe Wells in late afternoon. Turn right, back down the canyon. The next stop will be in 9 miles.

 About 1.5 miles down Grapevine Canyon from Scotty's Castle the road passes through a grove of cottonwood trees, a sure sign of shallow fresh water. The abundant springs and cooler temperatures at this 3,000-foot elevation were important factors in Johnson's choice of this area for his vacation ranch. Turn right at the mouth of the canyon, following the signs to Ubehebe Crater.

Ubehebe Crater

 **(65.6)** Besides flash floods and earthquakes, add volcanic eruptions to Death Valley's list of past cataclysms. Only a few thousand years ago, great explosive eruptions blasted out this half-mile wide, 600-foot deep crater. Molten rock rose along fractures and mixed with ground water in the alluvial fan deposits. The superheated water flashed to steam and blew out both the fan rocks and volcanic fragments called cinders.

Looking at the crater wall you can see the older fan deposits that are light in color in contrast to the darker beds of cinders that were dumped on top. The sudden change in color of the rocks about 150 feet below the rim marks the transition. Cinders were scattered over 6 square miles around the crater by the violent explosions, and form the dark gray soil that is now sparsely dotted with desert holly bushes.

Only the main crater is visible from the parking area, but by hiking up the rim to the right one can see several distinct craters. The flat area in the bottom of the main crater is a small playa formed by fine debris sliding and washing down from the crater walls.

Unless you have a tour booked at Scotty's Castle, return south in Death Valley toward Stove Pipe Wells. Reset your trip meter to zero, since by this distance no two indicators will agree. The next stop will be in 41.4 miles.

On the long drive down the length of Death Valley, notice how the road descends into the deeper, central portion of the valley, and the far mountains seem to disappear to some distant vanishing point. Imagine how overwhelming the vast scale and emptiness of this land must have been to humans on foot or horseback.

Pass by the gravel roads leading to the sand dunes, and at the highway intersection (38.8 miles) turn right toward Stove Pipe Wells.

Devil's Cornfield

(41.4) Pull into the parking area for a closer look at this almost surrealistic "cornfield". On both sides of the road are clumps of brush 4 to 10 feet tall that at first glance look like cornshocks. This is arrowweed, whose straight stems were sometimes used by Indians for arrow shafts. When rainfall has been above average this area becomes a saline marsh, and even during long dry spells salty ground water is not far beneath the surface. Arrowweed thrives where its roots can reach water that contains 0.5 to 3% dissolved salts, far above the limit for drinking water. When the ground is dry, wind slowly removes sand and soil, leaving the older bases of the arrowweed clumps perched above the present surface.

The next stop will be in 2.7 miles. Pull off

DEATH VALLEY WILDFLOWERS

A few wildflowers bloom in Death Valley in even the driest years, but with the right weather conditions the display can be truly spectacular. The requirements for heavy germination seem to be rainfall that is well above normal and spaced throughout the winter, combined with warm temperatures following the showers. When that happens, desertgold and evening primrose carpet the fans with yellow, while globemallow and poppies add splashes of orange. Desert fivespot, sandverbena and beavertail cactus provide accents of pink to magenta, and the ethereal white gravel ghost seems to float above them all. In dry washes you'll find everything from big bushes of desert rocknettle to mats of tiny "belly flowers"; from the beautiful sacred datura to the bizarre Rixford eriogonum that looks like a tiny pagoda made of rusty chickenwire. Wildflower bloom starts as early as February at the lower elevations; if you are in Death Valley in March or April try the mountain passes for later displays.

Beavertail cactus

Desert pricklepoppy

Desert fivespot

Whitemargin euphorbia

Mojave aster

Pebble pincushion

Mojave desert-star

Desert globemallow

Mojave hedgehog cactus

Desert rocknettle

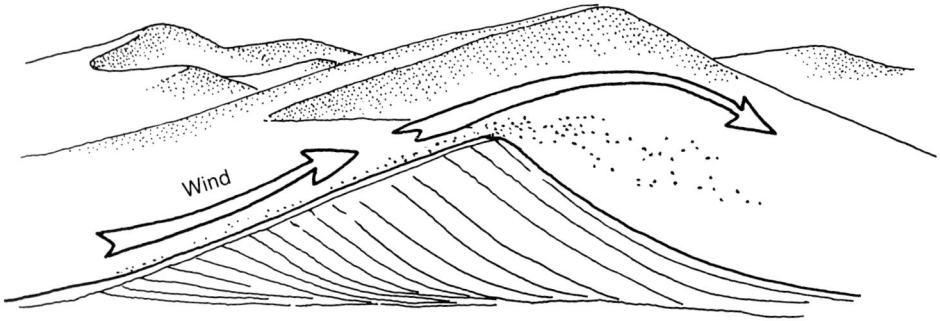

on the broad shoulder of the highway when you reach a roadside display where the sand dunes are close to the road.

Sand Dunes

(44.1) A booklet is usually available in a box near the display. Take one along and walk out onto the dunes for one of the best adventures in Death Valley.

These billowing dunes look like great ocean waves suddenly frozen in motion with their surfaces covered by complex patterns of smaller ripples. Pick up a few grains of sand. These tiny grains are pieces of rock, most of them fragments of quartz. More than a billion years ago one of these grains was perhaps part of a quartz crystal growing 5 miles below the Earth's surface as a great mass of granite cooled. Uplifted in an ancient mountain range, broken loose by wind and rain, and washed to some barren beach before the dawn of life, that grain may have become buried in a layer of sandstone and cemented into quartzite. Tilted into daylight again in a range flanking Death Valley, weathered out and washed down into an alluvial fan, the sand grain began to approach its present time and place. Wind picked up the grain and blew it down the valley. The wind slacked; the dust kept

blowing but the sand grain remained in this 14-square-mile field of dunes. It may have been buried and uncovered thousands of times as the wind shifted, increased or stilled. It and countless billions of other grains of sand dance into endless patterns. Each grain has its own history, many of them more complex than the sketch above.

Great areas of dunes called "sand seas" cover huge regions in Arabia and Africa, where some dunes are more than 1,000 feet high. These in Death Valley are closely related, although they are much smaller. What is needed for dunes to form is a source of sand, wind to winnow the sand and dust from the gravel, and then the dust from the sand. As the wind bounces the grains along into a drift, the cornice of the drift keeps collapsing into a steep slope called the slip face. That sliding slope is called the "angle of repose", which for sand is about 30 to 35 degrees.

In regions where the wind blows steadily from one direction the dunes are crescent-shaped or linear, and slowly migrate downwind. Here the wind is more variable and the dune pattern more complex.

The trees nestled in clumps among the lower dunes are mesquite. Their roots reach down through the dry sand into mildly saline ground water. Seeds from the mesquite feed kangaroo rats, whose burrows are common near the trees. Insects also eat seeds, and lizards and birds eat the insects. Snakes, birds of prey, foxes and coyotes hunt farther up on the food chain. The many tracks in the sand near the mesquite thickets attest to a complex web of life out here on the dunes.

Most of the creatures in Death Valley gather or hunt for food at night to avoid desert heat. Their tracks are probably the most you will see of them, but the dunes are a fine place to look for tracks — perhaps even those of the sidewinder rattlesnake, which leaves strange offset marks across the sand.

Even lizards stay out of the sun when they can. The largest lizard in Death Valley is the chuckwalla, which can reach a foot or more in length, and prefers rocky areas. It is not poisonous, and its main defense is to hide in a crevice and puff up its body to prevent being pulled out by an enemy. One fearsome-looking creature you might see at elevations of 1,000-3,000 feet, perhaps crossing a road, is the tarantula. With a large, dark hairy body and a 6-inch leg span this spider is an impressive sight, but is non-poisonous and considered harmless.

Bighorn sheep graze in the surrounding mountains, especially near springs, and the desert-wise coyote covers both basin and range in quest of food. The Indians living in the desert knew how difficult it was to stay alive; they had great respect for the crafty coyote, whom their legends say will be the last animal on Earth.

Notice the hard, patterned ground in some of the low spots among the dunes. These are mud layers that dry and shrink into a network of cracks.

The next and last stop will be in 2.1 miles.

Tracks across the sand

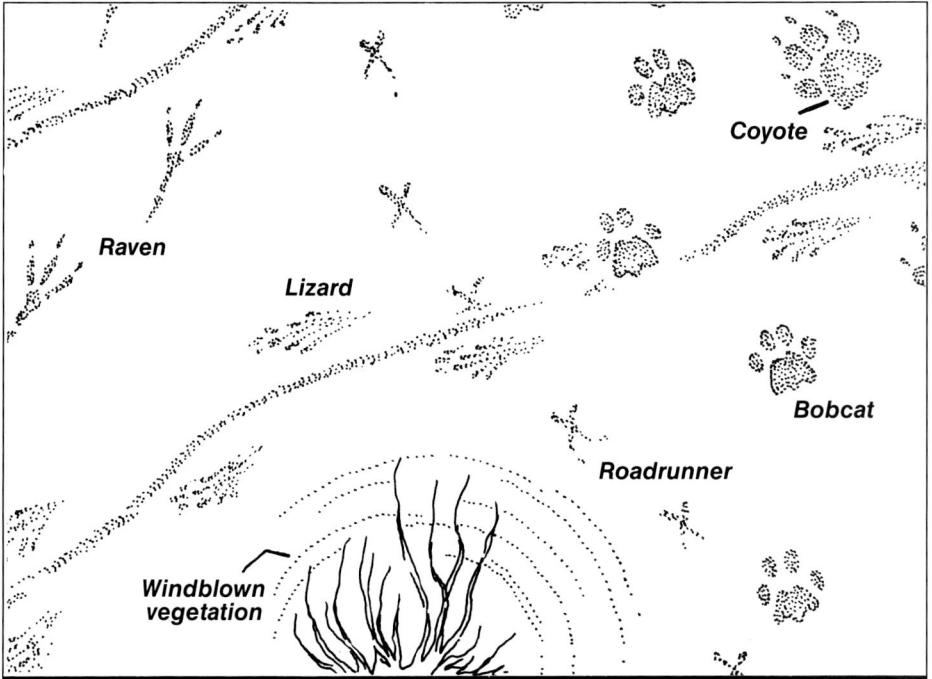

Coyote

Raven

Lizard

Bobcat

Roadrunner

Windblown vegetation

Desertgold

Sand dunes and Grapevine Mountains

Ubehebe Crater

Stove Pipe Wells

(46.2) This village was founded in 1926 as Death Valley's first tourist resort. The original "stovepipe well" is about 5 miles northeast on the other side of the dunes. Marked by an old piece of stovepipe sticking up beside the hand-dug well, it had long been used by travelers as a source of precious water. As the story goes, a developer had hoped to build a bungalow resort near there, but his lumber trucks became stuck in the sand at the present site of the village. The drivers unloaded the lumber to free the trucks, and it was decided that rather than reload it they would dig a well where they were. Luckily they struck water so they stayed, built a cluster of bungalows, and appropriated the name of the original well.

Near Stove Pipe Wells resort is a historical marker commemorating Burnt Wagons Point. The actual point is a few miles south of here, but it is part of the dramatic story of the first group of pioneers to cross Death Valley. At that camp one group of men killed their oxen and burned their wagons to dry the meat, before struggling out of the valley by what is now Towne Pass.

Death Valley is a land of extremes and of legends: record heat, lowest rainfall, deepest sink, lost gold, shimmering mirages. In yesterday's uncrowded world, wilderness was where people became lost. In today's world, wilderness is where you can find yourself.

SIDE TRIPS ON DIRT ROADS

The five trips listed here are on dirt roads that are periodically maintained, and suitable for a standard pickup truck or a passenger car with reasonably high clearance. On some occasions roads may be temporarily closed; check at the Furnace Creek Visitor Center before taking these fascinating side trips. Death Valley has many miles of very rough, four-wheel-drive roads that are not patrolled or maintained. These are not included in this section, but if you would like to know about them ask at the Visitor Center for a handout called Backcountry Roads.

Keane Wonder Mine
A short side road — 7 miles round trip — leads to the remains of a stamp mill that processed ore from the Keane Wonder Mine early in this century. Seventeen miles north of the Visitor Center on the Beatty Cutoff, this gravel road turns off to the right, crosses a dry wash and climbs an alluvial fan to the old mill site at the base of the Funeral Mountains. Ore was brought down from the mine to the mill by a mile-long tramway, parts of which are still visible on the steep mountainside. This side trip to the Keane Wonder Mill can be easily combined with the Titus Canyon drive.

Titus Canyon
The one-way drive through this isolated desert canyon is the best back-road trip in Death Valley. This rough, steep road begins just outside the park, 6 miles southwest of Beatty, Nevada off Highway 374. It crosses the Grapevine Mountains at Red Pass (5,240 feet) and drops down into Titus Canyon, following the dry bed of the canyon for 7 miles to its mouth in Death Valley. Colorful and contorted rock layers, the ghost town of Leadfield, Indian petroglyphs, and the final deep, narrow, winding canyon give a feeling of being in

Desert Textures

Mud cracks

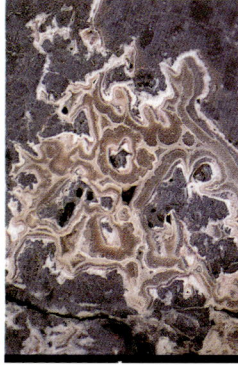
Crystals in cavity

Salt crystals

Salt flats

Marble

Tracks

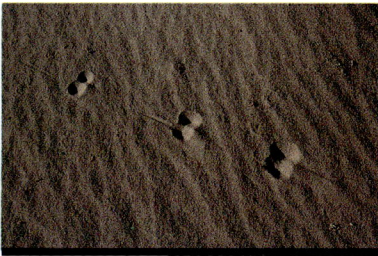
Tracks

Mud cracks

Mud cracks

Ripples and tracks

41

Petroglyph of bighorn sheep

another world in another time. The total distance on the dirt road back to the highway in Death Valley is about 26 miles, and the drive should be experienced in handling steep narrow roads. Allow at least a half-day or more for the round trip from Furnace Creek. This road is closed in summer because of heat and flash-flood danger, and to protect bighorn sheep.

West Side Road
This 34-mile-long road leaves the highway 6 miles south of Furnace Creek and follows the valley bottom along the west side of the playa, rejoining the highway near the south end of Death Valley. Three miles from its northern junction with the highway, the road crosses a stretch of beautifully patterned salt pan caused by cracking and salt recrystallization. Farther south, the road passes near Tule Spring where two of the 1849 emigrant families probably camped while waiting to be rescued. Notice the thickets of mesquite, which indicate ground water near the surface at the toes of alluvial fans. The sinking of Death Valley in this area occurs mainly on the east side — like a trap door hinged on the west side. The large fans on the west, compared to the smaller, largely-buried fans on the east side of the valley, are evidence of this downward tilting to the east. Just before the highway junction is a

ford across the usually (but not always) dry Amargosa River. The West Side Road rejoins the highway near the Jubilee Pass road. South of the junction is a hill called Shore Line Butte, where you can see a series of terraces that were cut into its sides by old shorelines of Lake Manly.

Aguereberry Point
The view into Death Valley from 6,430-foot-high Aguereberry Point is superb, though looking down on Furnace Creek from this perch gives even the steadiest a touch of vertigo. This part of the Panamint Range is composed of great upturned layers of quartzite. The 7-mile-long road to the point turns east from the paved road 10 miles north of Wildrose (see page 3).

About 1.5 miles after leaving the highway, the Aguereberry Point road passes by the old gold mine diggings of Harrisburg. There you will find some interpretive exhibits, and you may even want to take a flashlight and explore the old Eureka Mine tunnel which is open in spring.

Charcoal Kilns
A row of 10 large stone structures that look like giant beehives stand in the pinyon pine and juniper forest high on the west side of the Panamint Range. In the 1870's these kilns produced charcoal for silver mine smelters in the treeless Argus Range, 30 miles to the west. Wood from the sparse forest at 7,000 to 9,000 foot elevations in the Panamints was heated in these 30-foot-high kilns. Charcoal was made by preventing air from reaching the wood stacked above fires in the base of the kilns. Creosote and other volatiles were driven off rather than burned. Thousands of bushels of charcoal were hauled down the mountain every day, across Panamint Valley, and up to the silver mines. The road to the long-abandoned charcoal kilns climbs east into the mountains for 7 miles above Wildrose (see page 3). The first few miles are paved, the last are gravel.

HIKING TRAILS

There are hundreds of miles of open country and side canyons in Death Valley for the dedicated backpacker to explore on foot, but we recommend the following hikes for the visitor with just a little extra time. Be sure to carry drinking water, and be aware that flash floods are possible in desert canyons if a cloudburst occurs upstream. If you have not taken the Golden Canyon trail (described on page 21) or the Salt Creek trail (page 29), we recommend that you try one or both of them.

Titus Canyon

Take the 2-mile-long gravel road from the highway to the mouth of Titus canyon. Hiking up the narrow, twisting canyon you will see flood-polished rock walls with some areas of crystal-filled cavities, or places where fractured pieces of dark limestone have been surrounded by white crystalline cement. Flowers and plants flourish briefly in the dry stream bed after a rainstorm. Be alert for an occasional vehicle. Cars are allowed to drive down the canyon, but they are scarce until mid-morning.

Mosaic Canyon

A 3-mile-long gravel road up the fan behind Stove Pipe Wells leads to the trailhead of Mosaic Canyon. Carved into white marble and a mosaic of recemented stream gravels, this twisting canyon through polished rock walls is only a few feet wide in places. The first 3/4-mile-scramble up the gorge is the most scenic, but you can hike for about 2 miles in the upper branches of the canyon. Beware of climbing up dry waterfalls; they can be difficult to descend.

Natural Bridge

A 1.5-mile-long gravel road from the highway north of Badwater climbs up a steep fan to the canyon mouth. A one-half-mile hike up the dry stream bed leads to the 50-foot-high arch of a natural bridge. Erosion gullies on its north side show the old stream course before it tunneled through the bend to form the arch.

Wildrose Peak

Hiking in the high Panamint Range west of Death Valley is a good way to avoid the hot valley temperatures common from May to October. The trail to Wildrose Peak climbs 2,000 feet in four miles, through pinyon and limber pines, and the view from the 9,054 foot summit into the valley is spectacular. The trail begins at the Charcoal Kilns. Telescope Peak, the highest point in the park, is also accessible by a 7-mile-long trail from Mahogany Flat Campground, 2 miles beyond the Charcoal Kilns.

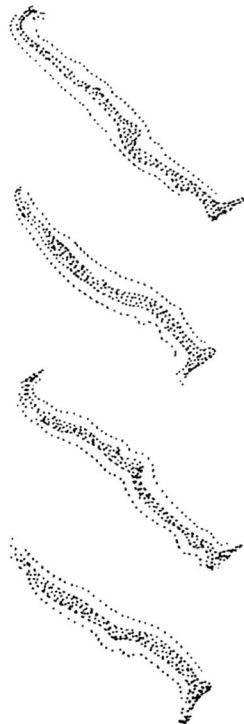

Sidewinder rattlesnake tracks

Scotty's Castle

Desert sky

Date palms

Charcoal kilns

FOOD AND LODGING

Accommodations
Furnace Creek Ranch — Open year-round
Furnace Creek Inn — Open October to May
    (Reservations for both — 619 786-2345)
Stove Pipe Wells — Open year-round
    (Reservations — 619 786-2387)
Panamint Springs Resort — Open year-round
    (Reservations — 702 482-7680)

Meals
Furnace Creek Ranch — Cafeteria, coffee shop, steak house, bar and snacks
Furnace Creek Inn — Dining room, supper club, bar, Sunday brunch
    (no meal service in summer)
Stove Pipe Wells — Dining room, bar
Panamint Springs Resort — Dining room, bar
Scotty's Castle — Snack bar

Picnic Supplies
Furnace Creek Ranch, Stove Pipe Wells, Panamint Springs Resort, Scotty's Castle

Campgrounds
Open all year — Furnace Creek, Mesquite Spring, Wildrose, Panamint Springs
Winter only — Texas Spring, Sunset, Stove Pipe Wells
Summer only — Emigrant, Mahogany Flat, Thorndike
    (For Panamint Springs campground
    information call 702 482-7680;
    for all others call 619 786-2331)

Barrel cactus

SUGGESTED READING

General

Gebhardt, Chuck, INSIDE DEATH VALLEY. Felton, CA: Big Trees Press, 1980.

Jaeger, Edmund C., THE CALIFORNIA DESERTS. Stanford, CA: Stanford University Press, 1965.

Jaeger, Edmund C., A NATURALIST'S DEATH VALLEY. San Bernardino, Inland Printers and Engravers, 1964.

Kirk, Ruth, EXPLORING DEATH VALLEY. Stanford, CA: Stanford University Press, 1981.

Larson, Peggy, THE DESERTS OF THE SOUTHWEST. San Francisco: Sierra Club Books, 1977.

Schad, Jerry, CALIFORNIA DESERTS. Helena, MT: Falcon Press, 1988.

Flora and Fauna

Bowers, Janice E. and Wignall, Brian, SHRUBS AND TREES OF THE SOUTHWEST DESERTS. Tucson, Southwest Parks and Monuments Association, 1993.

Dawson, E. Yale, CACTI OF CALIFORNIA. Berkeley, CA: University of California Press, 1982.

Dodge, Natt N., FLOWERS OF THE SOUTHWEST DESERTS. Globe, AZ: Southwest Parks and Monuments Association, 1973.

Ferris, Roxana S., DEATH VALLEY WILDFLOWERS. Death Valley, CA: Death Valley Natural History Association, 1983.

MacMahon, James A., DESERTS. The Audubon Society Nature Guides. New York: Alfred A. Knopf, Inc., 1985.

History

Austin, Mary, THE LAND OF LITTLE RAIN. Albuquerque, NM: University of New Mexico Press, 1974. Originally published in 1903.

Cornett, James W., DEATH VALLEY NATIONAL MONUMENT, A PICTORIAL HISTORY. Death Valley, CA: Death Valley Natural History Association, 1986.

Lingenfelter, Richard E., DEATH VALLEY AND THE AMARGOSA. Berkeley, CA: University of California Press, 1986.

Paher, Stanley W., SCOTTY'S CASTLE. Las Vegas, NV: KC Publications, 1985.

Geology

Collier, Michael, AN INTRODUCTION TO THE GEOLOGY OF DEATH VALLEY. Death Valley Natural History Association, 1990.

Hunt, Charles B., DEATH VALLEY: GEOLOGY, ECOLOGY, ARCHAEOLOGY. Berkeley, CA: University of California Press, 1975.

Sharp, Robert P., GEOLOGY FIELD GUIDE TO SOUTHERN CALIFORNIA. Dubuque, IA: Wm. C. Brown Company, 1972.

Maps

DEATH VALLEY NATIONAL PARK MAP. Evergreen, CO, Trails Illustrated, 1996.

GUIDE TO DEATH VALLEY NATIONAL PARK. Los Angeles, Automobile Club of Southern California, 1995.

PHOTO CREDITS

All photographs in this road guide were taken by the authors except for the following: p.8 (bottom) National Park Service; p.10 (top) National Park Service; p.11 (top) John S. Shelton; p.22 National Park Service Historical Collection; p.28 National Park Service Historical Collection; p.38 Ben Jones, M.D., (insert) National Park Service; p.44 (top) National Park Service.

Cholla

Sandstorm